I'm On Me Mobile

I'm On Me Mobile

An Irresistible Collection of True Mobile-Phone Conversations

by

Anton Rippon &
Andrew Ward

Robson Books

First published in Great Britain in 2000 by
Robson Books, 10 Blenheim Court, Brewery Road,
London N7 9NT

A member of the Chrysalis Group plc

Reprinted © 2000 Andy Ward and Anton Rippon

The right of Andy Ward and Anton Rippon to be
identified as authors of this work has been asserted by
them in accordance with the Copyright, Designs and
Patents Act 1988

British Library Cataloguing in Publication Data

A catalogue record for this title is available from the
British Library

ISBN 1 86105 330 4

Typeset by SX Composing DTP, Rayleigh, Essex
Printed by The Guernsey Press Co. Ltd, Guernsey,
Channel Islands

Acknowledgements

We are very grateful to the people who told us mobile-phone stories or pointed out newspaper items: Ian Alister, Jill Cairns, Robert Chapman, Graham Clark, Valerie Dingle, Vivien Doyle, Holly Hardy, Helen Heard-White, Winston Heard-White, Daniel Hoyle, Ilene Hoyle, Alan Jenkins, Lynn Jones, Diane Kaylor, Helen Kemp, Karen Kuehne, Rose Lonsdale, Beryl Lymer, Wendy Lynas, Kate Park, Al Partington, Jill Peay, Linda Proud, Arne Richards, Nicola Rippon, Pat Rippon, Tony Robinson, Geron Swann, Hiroko Tanaka, Florence Wallace, Richard Wallace, Frank Webster and Bob Wild. Newspaper items generally came from the *Guardian*, *The Times*, the *Daily Telegraph*, the *New York Times* and the *Washington Post*. We would like to thank the editors of the *Top Flat Picayune* for printing our request for stories and, most importantly, a special thank you to all the people we heard using mobile phones. At first they annoyed us. Then, when we realized that they were working for us, we grew to love them.

If you overhear a mobile-phone conversation that you feel should be included in a future collection of mobile-phone stories, please drop a note to Anton Rippon or Andrew Ward, c/o Robson Books, 10 Blenheim Court, Brewery Road, London, N7 9NT.

Contents

IMTS (Improved Mobile Telephone Service) suffered from call set-up delay, poor transmission, limited frequency reuse, and lack of service areas. IMTS was supplanted by Advanced Mobile Phone Service (AMPS) that operates in the 800- to 900-MHz range. AMPS overcame the limitations of IMTS and set the stage for the explosive growth of cellular service which continues today.

Nathan J Muller, *Mobile Telecommunications Factbook*, 1998

Introduction

One day in 1998, we met for that thing of the past — a face-to-face conversation without mobile phones.

'I got on a train for Cardiff the other day and sat in an empty carriage,' one of us started. 'Then a man got on and started smoking. So I moved to a non-smoker.'

'Uh-huh.'

'Then, one by one, four businessmen came into the non-smoker and sat nearby. All of them had mobile phones.'

'Did you move to a non-mobile-phoner?'

'Wish I could have done. I almost went back to the smoking carriage but in the end I stayed where I was.'

'Something like that happened to me. One day I was overhearing so many mobile-phone conversations that I couldn't hear the one next to me for the one three tables away.'

'We should write them down.'

'Ah-ha.'

So, over the next two years, we noted what we heard and spotted stories in the press. Then we asked our friends to recall their most memorable one-way mobile-phone conversations. And finally, we researched the stories that had appeared in newspapers. The outcome is this book.

When we started the project, we wondered whether we might have to invent a few conversations to have enough for a book. No way. The actual conversations were sufficiently creative in themselves; we have changed only the names of certain people and companies. Imagination has a place, however, because you will have to guess what was being said at the other end of the phone. It was even suggested to us that our one-way text could be used for teaching English as a foreign language – 'Fill in the missing spaces with sentences that make sense'.

As we moved further into our project, we realized that we were capturing a slice of society. Mobile phones have affected social behaviour. They have brought a new style of conversation, with its excessive turn-taking and need to define geographical location in opening sequences, and a new style of etiquette. We often felt that people seemed to be talking more to us than the person on the other end of their fuzzy line. We would find a secluded place and someone would come next to us and start talking. But if a person took pains to ensure privacy we would obviously respect that. In the overheards that follow, you can generally assume the person was talking in a loud voice.

Some of the lines we heard were surreal. If you recognize any of these from the other end, maybe you could drop us a line and let us know what was really going on. At the other extreme, some overheards were routine arrangements that were a sample of everyday life. We have included a few of these mundane ones at the request of a friend who is convinced she keeps on hearing exactly the same conversation: 'I'm on the train . . . the 5.30 . . . it gets in at 7.32 . . . see you then . . . okay.'

As you can see in this book, though, they are not all the same.

1

I'm on the Train

A young female student making a short train journey.

'Hello . . . I'm on a train going to uni . . . No, I'm on the train . . . If we get cut off it's because I've lost my signal . . . I said, "If I get cut off it's because I've lost my signal" . . . Hello . . . Hello . . . Hello . . . Hello . . .'

A power-dressed businesswoman on a train between Slough and Reading.

'Hello, it's Nicola . . . Yes, fine . . . Look, I need to ask a favour. I'm supposed to collect Fiona from her nursery in ten minutes but I've fallen asleep on the train and missed my stop . . . Yes, we've gone past Slough . . . No, I'm still on the train . . . Yes, I've got to go on to Reading and by the time I get back to Slough and get to the nursery they'll be closed . . . Do you think . . . Oh, you can . . .'

A young woman is snoozing on a train that is approaching Birmingham New Street station. A mobile phone rings in the far distance. Then the noise comes closer. She stirs and fishes deep in the long pocket of her camelhair coat for the phone.

'Hello . . . Oh, hello . . . Yes . . . I've got a bone to pick with you . . . Yes, when you left this morning . . . Hello . . . Hello . . . Hello . . . Oh, these tunnels . . .'

Man in a suit.

'And so I finally said to her, "Look, me boss, you secretary."'

Man in a suit.

'Is she a lion or a pussycat? . . . Yes . . . Uh-huh . . . Yes, well, a lion is a very admirable animal.'

Man in a suit.

'When you despatched the templates on the BBS figures I'm sure you said . . . In terms of people giving it their best shot are they sending all those things back to you? . . . Can I ask, I need to see, was it planned that people would just fill it in? . . . Marvellous . . . Okay . . . Could you somehow get a reminder out? . . . I'm presenting them the following Friday at the Business Operations Committee . . . Yes, how can I summarize it in, say, ten graphs . . . First I have to get the data in!

Man in a suit.

'Hello, yes, I'm about to own three flats which I will be renting out unfurnished. Some things will be there – curtains, fridges, washing machines – so I need to take out some form of contents cover for each of the premises . . . Yes, okay . . . Hello, yes, I'm about to own three flats which I will be renting out unfurnished. Some things will be there – curtains, fridges, washing machines – so I need to take out some form of contents cover for each of the premises . . . Oh, I see . . . Okay, if you could put me through? . . . Hello, yes, did they tell you what this was about . . . Right, I'll start again then: I'm about to own three flats which I will be renting out unfurnished. Some things will be there – curtains, fridges, washing machines. I need to take out some form of contents cover for each of the premises. I'm just trying to get some guidance on how you might deal with this . . . No, no, the buildings are already covered on a block policy, it's just a few contents . . . That sounds a wee bit more than I have, how might there be a way of doing this . . . Right . . . Right . . . Right . . . I'll give them a ring. Thanks a lot.

Bye-bye . . .'

The same businessman on the same train, moments later.

'Hello, yes, I'm about to own three flats which I will be renting out unfurnished. Some things will be there – curtains, fridges, washing machines – so I need to take out some form of contents cover for each of the premises . . . Yeah, if you could put me through . . . Hello, I'm about to own three flats . . . Etc., etc., etc . . .

Businessman on a crowded train.

I'm phoning from the office . . . Yes, I'm working late.'

A man in a suit is sitting at a table with three other people. Across the carriage sit four more people at another table. All seven people are within earshot. The man makes one call and arranges to meet his girlfriend that evening. He makes a second call and speaks to his wife.

"Look, I'm going to be working late tonight, so I'm going to stay in a hotel in London . . . No, I won't be able to get back . . . and I've got a meeting first thing tomorrow morning . . . Okay, see you tomorrow evening."

At this point the man leaves his mobile phone on the table and goes out of the carriage. The other people look at each other uneasily. One of them, a young woman, picks up the mobile phone and redials the last number.

"Look, you don't know me but I'm on a train and I've just heard your husband make his last two phone calls. He's not actually working tonight. He's meeting his girlfriend."

The woman puts the phone back on the table and turns to the man sitting next to her.

'Do you think I did right?' she asks.

'No,' says the man. 'But if you ever want a job anytime just give me your name and address.'

A man makes several calls in a loud, annoying voice. Several people ask him to stop but he continues to make his calls. A horn-player from a well-known symphony orchestra eventually goes up to him and says, 'Well, in that case, since you're talking so loudly on the mobile phone, you won't mind if I do a bit of horn-practising next to you.'

A young woman on a train between Leeds and York.

'Hi . . . I'm not there yet, I'm still here . . . I'll be there soon then, is that okay? . . .Where are you? . . . No, I'm here, I'm not there yet . . . Yeah, I'll let you know . . . No, when I get there I'll let you know, but meanwhile I'm still here.'

A man is speaking on his phone as the train approaches a station.

'We're just coming into, er . . . [he looks out of the window] . . . We're just coming to, errrrr . . .' Aside: 'Excuse me, where are we?' . . . Voice from background: 'We're on a train, you idiot.'

Self-important man on a train to London.

'It's George, I'm coming to London, I think we should meet. Why don't you come to my hotel and we can have dinner together . . . er, George . . . er, ah, George Freeman.'

A young woman makes the same phone call over and over again between London and Manchester. If she says it once, she says it twenty times.

'Hi, this is Michelle, I'm a casting director

from [a large television company] . . . I'm looking for an elderly Ukrainian lady who looks like the bark of a tree . . . It's for a wood-preservative advert . . . It's going to be a shot of a tree with this lady next to it . . . Are there any Ukrainian clubs nearby where we might find one?'

A man in his fifties is travelling on a four-hour train journey. He makes no calls himself and this is the only call he receives.

'Hello . . . No, you've got the wrong person . . . Who am I talking to, please? . . . Hello . . . Hello . . . Huh.'

A young businessman in a suit is dozing on an afternoon journey. Is he trying to sleep off a heavy lunch? A phone call wakes him from his doze.

'Hello . . . Oh, hello, mate, how are you? . . .

Yeah, tell me about it . . . I'm recovering . . . I said, "Recovering" . . . [louder] "Recovering" . . . [still louder] "Recovering" . . . I'll tell you the rest of the story later, not that there's much to tell . . . Definitely, mate, have a good one.'

The man returns to his doze. Five minutes later he receives a second call.

'Hello . . . Oh, hello, mate, how are you then? . . . Oh, sorry, Alan, I thought it was someone else . . . Yeah, it was a bit presumptuous of me to call you mate . . . How can I help? . . . Yeah . . . Yeah . . . Okay . . . What's your number there? . . . I'll do a company check and get back to you right away.'

The same man now makes his first call.

'Hello, this is Mike Spackman, this is mega-urgent, I've just had Alan Clark of the [large multinational company] on the phone and he's been put on hold for three minutes and he's a bit agitated . . . Can someone call him back? . . . [he repeats the name of the large multinational company] . . . They're a big customer so it's mega-urgent . . . I'm the account manager . . . Let me give you his number . . . It's mega-urgent.'

Like a lot of these mega-urgent situations, it then took several phone calls to sort out the problem. We'll spare you the five in this case.

A jazz musician had corresponded by e-mail with a man called Clayton Plant, a music agent looking to recruit more jazz musicians to his books. Nothing came of the interchange. A month later the musician is on a train when the man opposite him pulls out his mobile phone.

'Hello, I can I talk to Joe Hanson, please . . . Yes, my name's Clayton Plant . . .'

Clayton Plant is not a common name, thinks the musician. When the call is finished the musician introduces himself. The two men talk for three hours. The musician is now on the agency's books and has taken some work from them.

A man in his thirties.

'. . . Bene . . . Bene . . . Si . . . Ciao.'

We've included this as a reminder that there were many foreign-language conversations that we were unable to record. In some cases we were unable to identify the language.

A young woman on a Friday morning.

'It was uncomfortable but you make do with these things when it's just for one night . . . You do indeed . . .'

Man in his twenties on a Friday night.

'How's it going over there? . . . The birds? . . . From them or from you? . . . Hello . . . Hello . . . Huh, talking to myself.'

Young man receiving a call.

'Hello . . . Oh, hello, how are you then? . . . Yeah, fine . . . I'm in Cambridge tonight so I can't make it down . . . Is Lucy there? . . . Oh, she's in the shower . . . Okay then . . . Bye-bye.'

Man in a smart suit answering a call.

'So am I . . . Carry on . . . I didn't hear a word of that.'

Same man answering second call on the same train.

'Ian, let's try again . . . It's absolutely unfair, we've provided advice on change-management and training . . . oh.'

Same man in same smart suit answering third call on the same train.

'Let's have another go; if not we can talk later this morning . . .'

We are amazed at the mobile-phone conversations on trains that concern sensitive matters or confidential subjects. Nothing seems taboo. One example is the man with a pretentious manner on a crowded train to London. He is too far away to be described. He is just a loud voice halfway down the carriage, a voice that can be heard by about forty other people. While making one of his routine phone calls, early in the journey, he learns about the death of a work colleague — a woman called Lynette (not her real name). He asks details of the death and repeats them to his audience.

Then the man rings six or seven other people and (none too gently) breaks the news to them:

'Did you know that Lynette had died? . . . Yes . . . An aneurism killed her . . . I saw her a month ago and she wasn't looking well then . . . Her family took her away for a holiday just before she died . . .'

Finally, with the whole carriage still listening, he makes his last call.

'Did you know that Lynette had died? . . . [disappointed] Oh, you've heard.'

A young woman on the London Underground.

'Now, look, I've been trying to put this behind me . . . Now, look, that's not what we're into now . . . What we're into now, we need more space.'

Male teenager.

'Hello, it's Chris . . . Hello . . . Hello . . . Oh, I'll send him a message, it's easier.'

Male teenager.

'Hello . . . Hello . . . Is anybody there?'

A man on a train leaving St Pancras Station makes four loud calls in rapid succession. Each one is the same:

'Hello, it's Luke. I'm on the train. We're just leaving.'

After the fourth call, the man sitting next to him turns and says: 'Shall I tell you something, mate. That's the last bloody call you're making on that thing while you're sitting next to me.'

A young woman travelling on a tram is explaining to her friend about the break up of her relationship with a live-in boyfriend. The friend had obviously been living in the same house.

'No, I'm just leaving . . . Yeah . . . I'm not

giving him money . . . He's got my video-recorder . . . He can have that if he wants – it's stolen anyway . . . Yeah, he can get caught . . . He got up this morning and he was chatting away. I won't even speak to him though . . . I don't want to fall out with him . . . I'm finding another place . . . I've seen one advertised, sharing with two other fellahs . . . £60 a week . . . It's not through an agency either, so I don't have to pay a £70 agency fee . . . It's owned by a woman . . . she seems a posh woman, she asked me twenty questions about myself . . . I'll see her Friday but there's one catch – £450 deposit . . . I can't understand why she wants all that money, it's two months' rent . . . Six months' lease . . . Well, I've got £250 already . . . Well, I'll see what it's like . . . I only need another £200 because I've got a cheque for £240 . . . Another £200 . . . The deposit's £450 . . . Yeah, I've got £250 so I need £200 . . . No, I'm not going anywhere at the minute . . . You found what? . . . Oh yeah . . . was that in the top drawer . . . two pink ones? . . . Were they in my room? . . . right, see you later.'

31

Businessman amongst the background hum of the train and clanking noises.

'. . . No, no, I'm still here . . . I was just paying for my coffee . . .'

Businessman.

'It's an extension of the cash-and-wrap desk . . . Yes, okay . . . If you need anything else just let me know . . . I'll be on me mobile all day.'

Gaunt businessman in his forties, wearing a DDG Sports anorak in a cold carriage.

'I need somebody in a senior capacity to get me this information as soon as possible because Wayne has yet again failed to do his job . . . The engineers . . . I have not been told when they're going, when they'll arrive there . . . No, I can see you've got nobody in charge . . . Okay, my number is . . .'

Businessman.

'Can you ring me back because I'm on me mobile . . . Yes, call me back.'

Young woman.

'Hello . . . Hi . . . I'm okay . . . Going to Derby . . . Yeah, how are you? . . . You're better now . . . Pardon? . . . Yeah . . . No, no . . . Yeah . . . Call me back later then . . . Bye . . . All right . . . All right . . . All right then . . . Okay . . . All right then . . . Call me back whenever you're ready . . . Bye.'

A man in his forties. The table in front of him is laden with computer equipment.

'It's me again . . . I need to send a fax to JJ, could you give me the number . . .'

Young woman reading a women's magazine while answering phone.

'Hello . . . Somewhere or other . . . The train's just decided to stop . . . In the middle of nowhere . . .'

A young woman is fiddling with her phone . . . Then she answers a *William Tell Overture*.

'Hello . . . Did you send me a text message? . . . I've just got a text message saying, "Sarah, turn on your phone."'

Young blonde woman.

'Hey, I won a hundred points on that Vantage card, the scratch card . . .The other two got a thousand points on theirs . . . Yeah, I know . . .

Typical, isn't it?'

Young man.

'I phoned you up three times . . . I phoned you up and you weren't there, I phoned you up and no one answered, and I phoned you up and your Mum said you'd just gone out.'

Young woman.

'If he does then he's not that fantastic and you don't want him.'

While conducting research for this book, we attended plenty of impromptu mobile-phone concerts on trains. We heard 'Auld Lang Syne', Spice Girls tunes, the *Godfather* theme, Brandenburg Concertos, *Strangers in the Night* and enough

William Tell Overtures to last a lifetime. On one occasion one of us was very tempted to stand up in a train and ask a woman receiving her third incoming call if she'd like to dance to this one.

Mobile-phone companies have developed techniques for using the key pad to produce musical notes, including sharps, flats and rests. Computer-programming composers have provided templates for popular songs. We foresee a future FA Cup Final with 20,000 West Ham United supporters waving their claret-and-blue phones at Wembley while being conducted in a uniquely synchronized performance of 'I'm Forever Blowing Bubbles.'

The television-drama *Reckless* begins with Dr Owen Springer (Robson Green) borrowing a mobile phone from Anna Fairley (Francesca Annis) while travelling on a train from London to Manchester. This was the start of their affair. Have any real-life lovers met over a shared mobile phone?

A businessman in an exceptionally smart suit breaks off from making notes from the *Financial Times* to make a call.

'Hello, Jackie, can I call you in half an hour?'

He ends the call.

Very smartly dressed man in his fifties with short beard.

'. . . What about the fundamentals? . . . Let's put all the crap aside, what about this witness — There is no witness? . . . She was supposed to ask at the tribunal . . . What did they say? . . . Well, that's a lie . . . Would you politely tell her that that's a lie . . . I'll speak to her tomorrow or the day after . . . How can she say she has a witness when she hasn't produced a witness? . . . I can't believe this . . . phhhhheeeeewwwwweeeeeee . . . Something needs sorting out . . . This can't be right . . .

Can we sue her? . . . What about this ACAS biddy? . . . Another leech in the system . . . all right, I'll try to sort something out tomorrow . . . The trouble is now, with Brighton and Birmingham, who's going to do it, who's going to pick it all up? . . . Don't you ask . . . I'm ending this conversation now.'

A woman who is perhaps in her sixties but of course looks younger.

'Hi, Charles . . . We've just left Birmingham New Street . . . The train was late . . . I had to get off the train and carry my bags all the way up and down . . . I didn't have time . . . I just had to get on the train . . . Well, I don't care . . . Hello . . . Hello . . .'

A very cheerful man with a jolly, booming voice on a sunny day.

'. . . Right, that's fair enough . . . We will sort

that one out . . . No problem at all . . . We'll pick it up from Ipswich yard . . . Right, okey-doke . . . Will do . . . Will do.'

He immediately makes his next call.

'Good morning, Wendy, it's Russell, I've got some times for Jennifer . . . Monday and Tuesday eight till four . . . Wednesday 19.30 to 7.30 . . . Thursday 19.30 to, say, midnight . . . Righty-ho . . . Thank you very much.'

Three young men are travelling on the same train for over two hours. A fat railway time-table book is on the table and they are on first-name terms with the train manager. Here are some of their calls.

'Hello . . . Tonight . . . Seven-oh-five . . . Been out every day this week . . . the Pines . . . C37 . . . Newton Abbot . . . No, I had seven-oh-five instead . . . Out of Portsmouth . . . Seven-oh-six is out of Birmingham . . . Six-three-four's doing Birmingham . . . You're lucky, I was just charging the phone up . . . Are you going for that Skipton – Edinburgh on the fourth?'

B97, B98 and B99 are allocated . . . And seven-sixty? . . . One-five-eight's around the north-east, is it? . . . M31's showing as stock at Bristol . . . KO'd, is it? . . . K'd throughout . . . No driver.'

'Seventy-six's allocated. To Newcastle.'

'I'll see you on G14 then . . . I don't want to get back to Birmingham and find you've gone north.'

'Does M56 leave Penzance tomorrow? . . . Three times, isn't it? . . . Tomorrow . . . Twenty-two's at Penzance . . . Probably do the downtrip . . . Seven-sixty and six-three-four, what are they allocated? . . . Is it? . . . And then?'

'Where are you? . . . Yeah, it's five-eight-four . . . Yeah.'

'I'm in Stoke on seven-oh-five . . . No, no, seven-two-two's the Charter tomorrow . . . What does the engine do tomorrow? . . . Has it got two engines on, too?'

A man travelled regularly on the same train. His fellow passengers grew accustomed to his frequent mobile-phone calls. Then came the occasion when one of the other passengers needed to use a mobile phone in an emergency. She asked to use the man's phone and picked it up from the table. The phone was a plastic imitation.

2

I'm at the Station

Businesswoman on a cold platform.

'It's me . . . The train's on time . . . If you give them a ring at five I can pick it up on my way home . . . How's Gabby? . . . Hang on, I can't hear, they're making an announcement.'

Teenage schoolgirl in a waiting-room at Macclesfield railway station.

'Can you call me back, please . . . Am I at home? No, I'm at the railway station.'

The same teenager moments later.

'Hello, hello . . . Where am I? I'm still at the train station . . . Waiting for a train . . . Congleton . . . It's near Stoke . . . Yeah . . . Yeah

'. . . Janet's not coming because she can't be bothered . . . There'll be just the five of us . . . There's Kate, Charlotte, Hayley and Jackie . . . Can you hear me better now? . . . Wait a minute, I'm going out here . . . Is that better? . . . How many are you bringing? . . . How many, twelve? . . . Can you still hear me? . . . Hayley says she wants flowers, clothes and chocolates . . . Only joking . . . What are you going to get me then?'

Man on a station concourse.

'Did you get the message I left on your machine? . . . You did . . . No, that was it really.'

Businessman on a station concourse, holding a piece of paper (the agenda).

'I'd like an extra fifteen minutes on tele-workers in the afternoon session . . . No, she doesn't need that long . . . Then the section on parental leave, that can now be split into two . . . Maternity leave new rules and maternity leave old rules . . . Yeah . . . Make that "continuing at eleven" . . . That one should be "employers' views" . . . That will be good for the next time but for this one we're just going to have to run with what we've got . . . To be honest I'm not going to prepare this till the last minute . . . Going back to "flexibility", we need a handout on the fixed-term contracts directory . . . I understand you've taken over these things from Joanne . . .We're going to need joining instructions, handouts and list of helpers . . . As I said at the brainstorming session on Monday, on these courses there has to be a progression through the day or it makes no sense.'

Man on a concourse at five o'clock on a Wednesday afternoon.

'If you do it tonight you might be able to catch the Americas and Canada – they're on the same day.'

Young woman on the concourse.

'I'm just sort of hanging around now . . . All right then . . . Toodle-pip.'

Man in blue overalls in a waiting-room at 9.40 am.

'I'm stuck at the train station . . . Train's cancelled . . . Next one's 10.41 . . . I don't know, they've probably run out of coal or Casey Jones is still having his breakfast . . . I know, it's crap, isn't it? . . . It'll be a quarter to 12 or 12 o'clock . . . The train's coming in now but it's not going out . . . Awright then . . .'

Young man walking out of a railway station.

'I'm here now, where do you want me to go?'

Man in a grey suit standing on the railway-station platform.

'Hold on, why can't we run it? . . . We tested that the other day . . . I was stood with you when he came up and said it was all right . . . They've raised it, have they? . . . We're looking pretty bad on this, aren't we? . . . I left a message for Roger but he never got back . . . I left a message on his voice mail but he never got back to me . . . Just remind him that I left him a message . . . Monday, I think it was . . . Yeah, Monday . . . That's the only thing from my side of the fence . . . But the other thing is that they've changed the spec without any consultation, blah, blah, blah . . . The bottom line is, they didn't raise it with us earlier.

Young woman wearing platform heels on a platform on a Thursday afternoon.

'No, the train's coming . . . See you next Friday . . . No, no, a week tomorrow.'

Young woman outside a rail station under the canopy sheltering from the rain. While she speaks she is trying to attract the attention of a taxi.

'Hello . . . Hello . . . Hello . . . Hello . . . I can't hear you . . . I can't hear you . . . Hello . . . I couldn't hear you for a second . . . You want to talk to me? . . . Yes . . . You can talk to me if you want to . . .'

She dashes through the rain to a taxi.

A middle-aged businessman collects his brief-case as the train pulls into his station at 7.40 pm.

'Hi, honey . . . Listen, I got tied up at work, but we're just about to pull into Larchmont . . . Would you believe it? [turns to fellow travellers] she's on the same train.'

Young woman, crouching uncomfortably at the edge of a platform.

'Oh! I was going to leave you a message.'

Businessman collecting his coat ready to alight from the train at London Paddington Station.

'I'd better go now because the train's arrived at Paddington and if I don't get off I'll get swept up with all the rubbish.'

Young man in smart suit walking into the station.

'Nah, nah, it was a pretty good interview . . . Pretty friendly . . . I'll tell you what was funny, though . . . You know I said that she phoned last night and asked me, "Do you drive? Do you own a car?" She asked those questions again in the interview. I said, "Yes, yes."'

Young teenager standing at Oxford station looking at the information board.

'It stops at Reading, Basingstoke and then Winchester . . . Oh, I've just seen someone from school . . . See you later.'

He walks fifteen yards across the concourse and talks to another teenager.

A young woman is boarding a train with a large bag and a pushchair when her mobile phone rings. She puts the pushchair down on the top step and answers the phone.

'Can I phone you back? I'm just trying to get on the train.'

3

Guess Where I Am?

A man in a red T-shirt on the top of Shipman Head, Isles of Scilly.

'The psychic energy here is absolutely phenomenal.'

A defendant in Gloucester Magistrates' Court, facing a charge of handling stolen goods, January 1994.

'I can't talk now – I'm in the dock.'

The defendant was warned that by allowing his mobile phone to ring he was in contempt of court and risked a jail sentence.

A Methodist minister in a church in the north of England.

'Oh, hello, dear . . . Yes, I'm fine, but I'm in the middle of taking a service at the moment.'

A Quaker meeting has been silent for about ten minutes. Then a phone rings.

John Reinhard, an archaeologist, discovered three Inca mummies dating back to AD 1,500 while on a trip in Argentina. He used his mobile phone to call authorities in the local provincial capital and they were able to arrange a vehicle to carry cases containing dry ice to preserve his historic find.

(from *Iridium* in-house magazine August 1999)

In September 1998, Neil Whitehouse boarded a British Airways Boeing 737 flight from Madrid to Manchester. Whitehouse, a 28-year-old oil-worker from Mansfield, Nottinghamshire, refused to switch off his mobile phone despite repeated requests from the captain and the cabin crew. When the matter went to Manchester Crown Court, in June 1999, the court heard about the increasing number of reports from pilots of electromagnetic interference. Whitehouse was convicted of "recklessly and negligently" acting in a manner likely to endanger the flight. He was sentenced to 12 months in jail.

Fifteen-year-old schoolboy at the back of the class during a lesson in a West London secondary school.

'James Enterprises, how may I help you?'
(from *The Times*, 2 April 1999)

We have heard of one teacher who allows children in his class to take calls and then embarrasses them as much as possible: 'Alex has got a phone call, let's all listen to Alex answering his phone . . .'

In July 1997, *The Times* reporter Alan Hamilton was attempting to catch a British Midland flight to Edinburgh. The plane was leaving from Heathrow Airport but Hamilton had only got as far as Hammersmith with just five minutes before final check-in time. He phoned the departure desk.

'Do not sell my seat to a standby layabout. I am on my way, battling through acts of God and the London Tube.'

Hamilton arrived five minutes before departure time but his seat had been held.

(from *The Times*, 17 July 1997)

1999 Leeds Music Festival.

'Where are you? . . . Ah, you're in the information tent . . . I'm just in front of Wristband Exchange . . . Walk out of the information tent . . . Yes . . . Now look across . . . That's right, the one waving to you, the one with the mobile phone.'

We have heard a number of stories of phones dialling the emergency services by mistake. And there are stories of phones switching themselves on and redialling the last number. For instance, a man throws his bag with the phone in it in a taxi and unwittingly redials the last number as the bag lands, the mobile taking the impact. The last person called answers the new call and can hear a faint conversation between her caller and the taxi driver. Accidental redials have proved particularly problematic when the last call was to a live-in partner and the overheard conversation involves another lover.

In October 1996 Tessa Jowell's phone rang during a speech by Health Minister Stephen Dorrell in the House of Commons. The Speaker, Betty Boothroyd, had already made it clear that phones should be turned off in the Chamber. (Visitors to the Strangers Gallery are not permitted to take in phones either.) The Deputy Speaker, Dame Janet Fookes, said, 'The Speaker has very strong views about modern technology. It should not be heard in this Chamber.'

In March 1998, Michael Heseltine's phone rang while he was making a speech in the House of Commons. Heseltine couldn't understand where the noise was coming from. He looked around the Chamber and suddenly realized it was coming from his pocket.

A mobile phone rang in Nottingham Crematorium during a funeral service in July 1997. A man stood up from his seat in the congregation and went to the back corner of the chapel, where he stood talking loudly as the service continued. Members of the congregation turned towards him and said 'Shush', but the man merely turned his back and continued his conversation. A hefty young man then sprang from his seat, grabbed the talker and threw him out the side door.

(from *The Times*, 24 July 1997)

A funeral in western Poland. The mourners stand by the graveside, looking down at the coffin. Then a phone rings from inside the coffin. One woman faints at the graveside. Other mourners leave in haste. The phone had been interred with its owner.

During a tennis match between Nathalie Tauziat and Anna Kournikova at Eastbourne in July 1999, a mobile phone went off in the crowd just as Tauziat was serving. There was a delay as the umpire announced that mobile phones should be switched off. There was a further delay when the crowd applauded the umpire's announcement.

Freelance cameraman Vaughan Smith had his life saved by his mobile phone when he was working for the BBC in Kosova in July 1998. He was in a group that came under fire from a sniper, and felt himself hit by one of the rounds but was able to continue. When Smith returned to the hotel he inspected the damage He was heavily bruised and bleeding, but his mobile phone, wrapped in a handkerchief, was wrecked. He assumed at first that he must have fallen on it when he dived for cover. Then he discovered a bullet inside the handkerchief: the sniper had hit the phone. Not surprisingly, it no longer worked and had to be replaced.

(from The Times, 1 July 1998)

Colin Stewart, United Nations political officer, speaking on his mobile phone in Dili, East Timor, while being interviewed by Maggie O'Kane of the Guardian, 16 September 1999.

'We've had calls saying that the refugee camps are being dominated by the militia. The callers are reporting violence, intimidation and executions in the camps. The militia are coming into camps with lists and calling out certain people, most of them young men, and taking them away. But generally there's a feeling that if people can hang on things will be okay. A couple of days ago the militia were shooting at our cars; but they are now confining themselves to rude gestures. They have looted everything by now.'

A police officer in Colombo, Sri Lanka, giving an interview to the New York Times on 15 October 1999.

'Looks like some people have got into the World Trade Center and begun shooting.'

The world's largest hedge maze is at Longleat in Wiltshire. It covers 1.48 acres and has 1.69 miles of pathways.

'I'm in your maze, I need to get out . . . Can you come and help me? . . . How do I get out?'

Sometimes families take different routes through the maze. Then they all get lost and phone one another.

'Where are you? . . . I'm jumping up and down: can you see me over the hedge?'

Helen Wilton (base camp) to Rob Hall (stranded on Mount Everest at 28,700 feet) at 9 am on 11 May 1996.

'Rob, this is Helen at Base Camp. You think about that little baby of yours. You're going to see its face in a couple of months, so keep on going.'

Guy Cotter to Rob Hall at 3.20 pm the same day.

'Rob, get moving down the ridge . . . thing is, mate, the lads who went up today encountered some high winds and had to turn around, so we think your best shot is to move lower . . . You're a tough man, Big Guy, we'll send some boys up to you in the morning.'

Rob Hall to his pregnant partner, Jan Arnold, at 6.20 pm the same day.

'Hi, my sweetheart. I hope you're tucked up in a nice warm bed. How are you doing? . . . In the context of the altitude, the setting, I'm reasonably comfortable . . . I haven't taken me boots off to check, but I think I may have a bit of frostbite . . . [and before signing off] I love you. Sleep well, my sweetheart. Please don't worry too much.'

There would be the last words anyone would hear Rob Hall speak. He died later that day. (Jon Krakauer, *Into Thin Air* (Macmillan) 1997

Tim and Jenny take their mobile phones wherever they go. One day they were walking along a beach on the West Wales coast. Tim's phone was in their rucksack and Jenny's in her handbag. Later, Jenny couldn't find her handbag anywhere. She phoned Tim's mobile phone. No reply. That's odd, she thought, knowing he usually kept it switched on. She phoned his house and phoned her own house to leave messages. Tim then phoned Jenny at her various numbers and eventually spoke to her at work.

'I can't find my mobile anywhere,' he says. 'Have you got it?'

Then Jenny's daughter phones Jenny at work.

'I think your mobile's just rung but I can't find it,' she says.

Jenny phones her own mobile number and then rings her daughter. Her daughter has not heard anything.

Later that day, Tim leaves a message on Jenny's answerphone at home: 'I've found your handbag – it was in the boot of my car.'

And then it finally dawns on Jenny. She phones Tim's mobile number and hears it ring in her own house. Then she finds the rucksack . . .

In January 1996, the Israeli Sin Bet murdered a Palestinian bombmaker, Yahya Ayyash, by wiring his mobile with plastic explosive and then ringing him. Yahya Ayyash was being held responsible for introducing suicide bombing tactics. At his funeral Hamar leaders took the decision to retaliate. This led to a campaign of suicide bombings in Israel.

Young man taking a call in the Lake District.

'Hello . . . Hi, Jamie . . . Where are you? . . . You're sick? . . . Oh, dear, what's the matter? . . . Well, actually, I'm on the summit of Helvellyn.'

Chung Chi-cheung was in a Hong Kong hospital having an operation to remove a growth on his colon. He was not under general anaesthetic so he was able to hear the surgeon using his hands-free mobile phone to talk to a car salesman. When Chung complained, the hospital authority apologized for the 'unpleasant experience'. They suspended the doctor and investigated the matter.

(from the *Las Vegas Sun*, 27 October 1999)

Woman at Macarran International Airport, Las Vegas.

'Sure we saw the Grand Canyon, but do

y'know what? It wasn't nearly so big as we'd been led to believe.'

A solicitor in South Shields, Northumbria, reported his mobile phone missing one day in May 1999. Police dialled its number and heard it ringing in a nearby cell – it was the cell occupied by the solicitor's client.

After a two-week trial at Sheffield Crown Court in January 1999, 61-year-old Ken Richardson was convicted of arranging an arson attack on the main stand of Doncaster Rovers Football Club. Richardson was the owner of the club at the time of the attack.

Richardson had hired a self-proclaimed ex-SAS trooper, Alan Kristiansen, to burn the stand as part of a property development scam. Unfortunately Kristiansen left his mobile phone at the burnt-out stand. The police easily traced the last call made on it – it was to

Richardson. Then they discovered the message on Richardson's answering machine:

'The job's been done.'

In February 1999, a classical music concert in China was abandoned after disruption from members of the audience using mobile phones. The Juilliard String Quartet brought their performance to a halt when the noise of ringing mobile phones and bleeping pagers proved too much to compete with.

(from John Gittings, in the *Guardian*, 23 February 1999)

Denver school pupil talking to a television station after a group of gunmen with automatic weapons and grenades had wounded a number of children in an attack on the school.

'I heard shots, and bullets were ricocheting off

lockers. I heard an explosion. There were students running. There were teachers running. It was chaotic.'

A woman went to the swimming pool. She changed into swimwear and walked through to the pool carrying her mobile phone and a towel. She left the phone and the towel at the side of the pool and started swimming lengths. The phone rang twice. Each time she swam to the phone, dried her hands and took the call while treading water.

(from Simon Hoggart, in *the Guardian*, 24 April 1999)

Man talking in a loud voice at Southampton Cricket Ground.

'Hello, it's Stephen here . . . I'm not sure whether I locked the garage door . . . Yes . . . Would you mind popping round the corner and checking for me . . . You'll find the keys in the usual place . . . Yes, I think I locked it but it pays to check . . . Oh, I'm going to have to go now, the umpire's coming over to talk to me.'

A report in the *Guardian* (30 September 1999) described a confrontation at the Labour Party Conference at Bournemouth. During an argument between Joe McCrea, a member of then Minister of Health Frank Dobson's staff, and a Channel 4 reporter, a photographer held out his mobile phone, shouting at McCrea, 'You're on Radio Five Live.' McCrea responded by smashing the phone.

Pigeon fanciers are worried that radio waves emitted by mobile phone masts might be interfering with the homing instincts of the birds. Pigeons navigate using the sun and the earth's magnetic fields. However, some scientists argue that the power of radio waves from mobile phone transmitters is small compared with existing television and radio transmitters.

In Lympne, Kent, in September 1999, a man was chased up a tree by a wild boar. Cowering in terror, he dialled 999 from the top of the tree. The police came and rescued him.

Young woman walking across a university campus.

'But, come off it, he's gorgeous.'

Man at the top of Mount Snowdon. The conditions are misty but the caller can see the expressions on the faces nearby. He is not at all self-conscious.

'I think I'm beginning to annoy people.'

A woman in her forties, standing at a stall in an antiques fair.

'You're not speaking into the phone right . . . No, that's better . . . You weren't speaking into it right, you'd got it away from your face . . .'

Writing in *She* magazine (September 1999), Saul Barry tells of how he dreams of a world without mobile phones called NoMoPho: 'In NoMoPho, train journeys would be just like they are in that "Sleepy time" advert with games of chess and snoozy penguins . . . I dream that I will never again hear a man order a Chinese takeaway in the middle of a film at the cinema nor witness the bizarre sight of a woman puffing away on a treadmill at the gym, ear glued to her mobile, wheezing, "57 calories, Jackie, and counting."'

The first country to have more mobile phones than traditional fixed-line units was Finland. In one café in Helsinki, a waitress takes the orders and communicates them to the kitchen, 15 yards away, by mobile phone.

(from T R Reid, in the *Washington Post*, 26 May 1999)

Hamish McRae, writing in the *Independent* (30 September 1999), quotes a story reporting that mobile phones in Finland have reached 110 per cent of the 18-to-25 age group. (Apparently quite a lot of Finnish youths have two phones.) Writes McRae: 'There are a couple of soft-drink machines in Helsinki which will give you a can of Coke if you tap in a few digits into your phone – the cost of the can appears on your phone bill the next month. A bank there has a system telling account holders of their nearest cash dispenser. Because the phone knows what cell it

71

is in and cells in cities are very small, the phone can direct the user to the machine without even needing to display a map.'

After watching a film in a cinema, are you one of those people who study every inch of the credits, looking to spot a familiar key-grip or animal-trainer? Aficionados of on-set catering will be familiar with names like Cecil B de Meals on Wheels and The Shooting Break. On 30 November 1997, in the *New York Times*, Eric Asimov wrote an original food review which focused on four on-set catering companies. At one location, he praised the breakfast burrito, a flour tortilla stuffed with eggs and anything else, like bacon or avocado. He wrote: 'You can eat it in one hand, and hold a cellular phone in the other. You just have to remember which one to bite.'

Runner at the finish of the New York Marathon.

'Hi, honey, I've done it . . . I'll be home in fifteen minutes.'

Scanning mobile-phone calls has proved an advantage to international spies. In January 1999 US officials confirmed that Washington had sent an American spy into Iraq to plant an eavesdropping system that intercepted mobile-phone conversations between Iraqi leaders.

Imagine the tension during the opening-night screening of Gus Van Sant's remake of the classic Hitchcock film *Psycho*. The cinema is full. Everyone is bracing themselves for the famous shower scene. It's coming up . . . this is the build-up . . . you can feel the tension in the cinema . . . and then one member of the audience decides to make a loud mobile-phone call.

(from Janet Maslin, in the *New York Times*, 5 December 1998)

One day in May 1998, 24-year-old Heath Hess was out walking and talking in Hornell, New Jersey, with a finger in one ear and a mobile phone clamped to the other. His stroll took him to the railroad tracks and he started wandering up the line. A big freight train loomed up behind him but Hess didn't hear it. The engine driver saw Hess and sounded his horn. Hess still didn't react. The engine driver applied the brakes and tried everything he knew to attract the caller's attention. As a last resort he jumped out of the engine and threw a water-bottle at the man. The train bumped Hess off the track, but fortunately he escaped with scrapes and bruises.

A Brooklyn man posing as a taxi driver unsuccessfully tried to rape a woman whom he had picked up as a fare. As the woman escaped, she grabbed the man's mobile phone. Police checked numbers in the phone's memory and laid a trap for the man at his girlfriend's house.

During UK Prime Minister Tony Blair's visit to South Africa, in January 1999, 22-year-old Linn Murray was reporting for the South African Broadcasting Corporation's Radio News. An angry crowd, organized by Muslims Against Global Oppression, broke through security, and police opened fire to disperse them. Murray was one of four people injured in the firing but she was still intent on filing her report. Lying on her back with her head supported by pillows and medical staff treating injuries to her legs, she described what had happened on her mobile phone.

During the 1999 Cricket World Cup match between South Africa and India, at Hove, Sussex, the two senior South African players, Hansie Cronje and Allan Donald, took the field wearing radio earpieces. Their coach, Bob Woolmer, had noticed the appearance of mobile communication between coach and participant in sports such as cycling. Woolmer talked to Cronje and Donald during the match and offered them options . . . but only until the first drinks interval. Then the match referee told the players to remove the earpieces. South Africa won the match by four wickets.

During one week, in June 1998, two rescue operations were launched by mobile-phone calls from Mount Rainier, USA. In the first incident, one person was killed and five injured by an avalanche. A woman phoned to report eleven people swept over Disappointment Cleaver. Her call cut hours from the response time. In the second incident, two climbers sounded the alarm after being caught in bad weather at 13,600 feet. Mountain-rescue services stress, however, that mobiles and other computer systems should not be seen as substitutes for proper navigation methods in remote areas because batteries can fail and equipment can be defeated by weather conditions or the terrain.

Young man in the toilets of a university library at 1.30 pm.

'Yeah, I've had a baguette . . . I'm just on my way in.'

A man in his forties outside the Royal Courts of Justice, The Strand, London.

'What happened was that the judge has agreed to allow his other allegation to be put before the jury.'

Blackpool has the largest roller-coaster in the world – "The Big One". For four seconds of the ride there is a near-vertical drop. Those must be the longest four seconds imaginable. Mobile phones are banned from the ride, presumably because they might interfere with the computer equipment. But who would want to use a mobile phone while screaming?

Man walking up and down in a secondhand bookshop.

'You don't want that Shakespeare, do you? . . . If you don't want it, give it me back and I'll put it into auction.'

4

I've Not Gone Far

When receiving an unwanted call from a mobile phone, one common tactic is to say 'You're breaking up' and then go quiet and finally hang up. A computer software engineer took this a stage further. He recorded the sound of mobile-phone interference and created an appropriate icon on his computer to call up the sound. When his boss rang in on a mobile phone, the engineer would click on the interference icon, hold the phone to the computer and say, 'You're breaking up.'

On 6 June 1994, The Times published a letter from Mr. R.G. Maling of Aylesbury, Bucks. Mr Maling described an incident in his local fitness group when a fitness fanatic jumped up

from his rowing machine to answer his mobile phone. As he did so, he tore a ligament in his back. *Mobile phone renders fitness fanatic immobile.*

A young man lying in bed.

'What are you doing on my phone?'

Woman in an office.

'Hello . . . Oh, can I phone you back in a minute? I'm on the other phone.'

Extract from a liturgy written by Canon Giles of St Paul's Cathedral, December 1998.

'Heavenly Father, in your great mercy you have given us this phone for the good use and benefit of all the people. Bless it and all its users in your service. Speak gently in the ears of those who employ it, turn all your words to prayers in your ears and connect them with us, and you, and the Holy Spirit.'

Scientists are still investigating whether mobile-phone use is related the brain tumours, cancer, increased blood pressure, poor short-term memory and concentration lapses. On 27 September 1999, the *Daily Telegraph* published a letter from Michael Blackstaff, Winchester, Hants, who claimed that mobile phones were a health hazard because they raised his blood pressure to dangerously high levels.

A husband and wife lost their mobile phone and decided to dial the number. The phone rang in the dog. The phone was passed four days later and was found to be in good working order. Don't even ask.

Vodafone customer care service once had a call from a man who could make outgoing calls on his mobile phone but couldn't receive incoming calls. When his phone was switched on, callers got a message saying it was switched off. It turned out that the problem arose through an occasion when he had been out drinking with some friends. As a practical joke, his phone was swapped with an identical phone belonging to a friend. His mobile phone was therefore in a friend's pocket. Switched off.

(from the *Daily Telegraph*, 15 October 1997)

In Sagamihara, Japan, a man called Saburo Masaoka uses mobile phones for his gold-panning business. Every cell phone contains a minute quantity of gold, used to fix silicon chips to the phone's computer circuit box. Masaoka's company, Yokohama Metal, buys discarded phones from major companies in their thousands. The phones are crushed and incinerated. The ash is heated, melted, bathed in acid and treated with chemicals so that the gold and silver can be refined in pure form. It takes about 70,000 phones to yield a 2.2-pound bar of gold. In five years, the company has turned more than 10 million discarded cell phones into gold bars.

(from the *Seattle Times*, 29 December 1998)

The disposal of used mobile phones is becoming an important environmental issue, with particular concerns about phone batteries. Certain countries have arranged recycling collection points. Sam Burton wrote to the editor of the *New York Times* (23 July 1998) to suggest distributing outmoded cellular phones without charge to interested segments of the schizophrenic-homeless population. Walking the streets shouting into the phones rather than into thin air would allow the schizophrenic-homeless to appear no more insane than the well-off thousands doing the same. Or no more sane.

Japanese scientists have invented tiny 'pet mobiles' that can be slipped under a pet's collar and activated without buttons. This will allow owners to phone their pets and say, 'Who's a good boy then?'

A Liverpool heroin and cocaine wholesaler is talking to one of his gang. The police are recording the conversation as part of an investigation into the whole operation. They happen upon corruption by a member of their own force, Detective Chief Inspector Elmore Davies.

'Can't we do anything to help him? . . . What bizzies can we get to? . . . Elmore? Elly? What kind of a fucking name is that? Offer the middleman two grand and see what happens.'

Davies was later sentenced to five years in prison.

Woman at home.

'Hello . . . I'm about to go in the shower . . . Why did you ring me on the mobile, I'm at home? . . . You could have rung me on the landline . . . No, I don't take my mobile in the shower . . .'

One of the major drawbacks of mobile phones is their susceptibility to eavesdropping. A number of high-profile cases have focused on the illegal use of scanners to record private mobile-phone conversations. Sometimes these recordings have also been made available to newspapers. The Prince of Wales and the late Princess of Wales both made calls to their respective paramours that were later published. In the United States, a Florida couple recorded a conference call between Newt Gingrich, Republican Leader of the House of Representatives, and other leading Republicans. They were discussing how to react to ethics-committee charges against Gingrich. The Florida couple, John and Alice Martin, were each fined $500. But according to the US Supreme Court, people conversing on cordless phones of all sorts can have no expectation of privacy.

Our book is not for the purpose of advising you on how to get the best out of your mobile phone. That information is available in a book called *Mobile Phones – The Tricks of the Trade* by Phil Jones (Interproducts, Perth, Scotland, 1997). If you want to know how to save money and get the best out of programming your phone, consult Jones the Phones.

Peter Laufer, author of *Wireless Etiquette: A Guide to the Changing World of Instant Communication* (Omnipoint, 1999), offers a number of etiquette rules for mobile-phone users. They include:

- use mobile phones sparingly in small, enclosed public spaces.

- give 'in-the-flesh' companions priority over a telephone call.

- don't shout or engage in 'loud and animated' conversations that disturb others.

- resist the temptation to borrow someone else's mobile phone.

5

I'm On the Road

Heard on a radio phone-in programme.

'I'm on the motorway . . . Yes, that's right . . .
Oh, God, I'm being pulled up by the police . . .
Oh, I'm on the hard shoulder now . . .'

Carol Pattinson was 32 years old when she
died in a car accident in Scotland in
September 1996. Her husband, Richard, was
seriously injured. The accident was caused by
a lorry driver losing control of his vehicle
while trying to hang up a mobile phone in
his cab. The lorry crashed into a line of slow-
moving traffic at a contraflow on the M8 and
shunted several cars into each other. The
lorry driver was fined £250 and given six

penalty points on his licence after admitting careless driving.

Woman driving on the motorway.

'Hang on a minute, Jill, I'll just have to steer for a bit now.'

In September 1995, a member of the public reported seeing a motorist wielding a handgun in London's West End. Scotland Yard's armed response unit surrounded the car with Heckler and Koch MP5 semi-automatic guns and the two occupants were forced into passive positions. One man lay spreadeagled face-down on the street; the other was pressed against railings. The two men were trussed up and taken into a police van. After 30 minutes the men left the police van laughing and joking. Yes, you've guessed. It wasn't a handgun after all – it was a mobile phone. At times guns and mobile phones look very similar, especially when carried in hip holsters or shoulder harnesses.

Shortly after this incident a Glasgow man wrote to *The Times* to congratulate the police on their decisive action against the menace of mobile telephones.

A drunken man travelling on a bus answers his phone at 9.30 pm on a Sunday evening.

'Wadderyehwant? . . . Yeah . . . Ugh . . . King's Arms . . . Budweiser . . . See ya later.'

In May 1997, a 35-year-old marketing manager, Peter Mill, was convicted of causing a fatal accident near Bracknell, Berkshire, by letting his car wander and collide head-on with a van on the other side of the road. The van driver was killed and Mill was seriously injured. The prosecution produced evidence to suggest that the marketing manager had been listening to messages left on his mobile phone at the time of the crash. The defendant denied this, but his telephone bill showed a 23-second call to his message service with no end signal. Also, police had a record of the time of the 999 call made by another driver on his mobile phone. The judge, however, said that it was speculation whether Mill was still on the telephone or had finished his call.

Mill was jailed for six months and banned from driving for two years for causing death by dangerous driving. The van driver's widow said: "I would hope that the media coverage of this case would help to make people more aware of the dangers of using a hand-held phone while driving. A car is not an office. Making calls while at the wheel of a car puts other people's lives at risk."

A young student is travelling on a bus at the start of a new university year. She holds her new mobile phone to her ear and speaks with an excited voice:

'Oh, someone's left me a message.'

Her excitement quickly turned to frustration, however, as she was unable to work out how to listen to the message.

In September 1996 an 11-year-old schoolgirl was killed in an accident at Pucklechurch, near Bristol. Rebekka Hudd was cycling home when she was knocked down by a four-wheel-drive Mitsubishi Shogun driven by a financial adviser, David Powell, who was talking to his wife on a mobile phone. The man, who admitted careless driving, was fined £250 and given six penalty points. The girl's mother said: 'There should be something on all cars which jams the signal on mobile phones so that they can't be used while the engine is on.'

A young man is sitting near the back of a bus. Wearing a fashionable suit and sporting a fresh haircut, he is groomed as if for an interview. He walks to the front of the bus, talks to the driver and then chooses a seat just behind the driver. He takes out his mobile phone and makes a call.

'. . . Yes, I was assured that the bus would arrive at 10.37 but it's now about ten minutes after that . . . I think I'm quite close now . . . ['This is it, mate,' shouts the bus-driver] . . . Ah, apparently I'm here.'

In October 1996, Kate Alderson, a 28-year-old *Times* reporter in the North West, was killed in a car accident in Cheshire. She was driving to the scene of a helicopter crash in which Matthew Harding, the chairman of Chelsea Football Club, and four others had been killed. Alderson had made two calls on her mobile phone to Peter Beal, of the Press Association, to ask for directions. A witness said that Alderson made a right turn across traffic while holding her mobile phone to her right ear with her right hand. As she made the turn she was hit by a car travelling at over 60 miles per hour on the Middlewich to Northwich road.

Cheshire coroner John Hibbert said: 'It is clearly dangerous to be using a phone or to have a phone close to one's ear while attempting to steer by one hand alone.'

In February 1998, a car belonging to David Withers was broken into and a number of items were stolen, including a pager. Using his mobile phone Withers left a message on the pager: 'Congratulations, you have won £500.' He left his mobile-phone number for the 'winner' to ring.

Unbelievably Withers received a call on his mobile phone. Withers told the man that he had won £500 in a church fête and had been paged because it wasn't safe to send the money through the post. Could the man come and collect it? The man got really excited and they arranged a meeting. When 24-year-old Justin Clark turned up to collect his prize he was arrested.

One foggy morning, at 7 am, 19-year-old Amber Scott, a student at Ball State University, Indiana, set out from her home in Anderson, Indiana, driving a Pontiac Grand-Am. She stopped for red lights at a railway crossing. She looked in her rearview mirror and saw a pick-up truck coming up too fast behind. The truck hit her car and knocked it forward just as a freight train was passing. The bonnet of the car wedged under the 33rd wagon of the train and Amber Scott's car was dragged along for more than three and a half miles with sparks flying. During the journey she pulled out her mobile phone and called home.

'Mom, Mom! I've been hit.'

The line went dead. Next she called the police.

'Some guy has hit me and I'm being dragged along by a train. Oh, please help me, please help me.'

After seven minutes she was knocked clear of the train by a sign beside the track. She escaped with cuts and bruises. The car was a write-off.
(from Michael Ellison, in the Guardian, 5 April 1999)

It was 3.30 am one July morning when a car driven by 18-year-old Rebecca Richards missed a sharp bend in Freathy, Cornwall. The car plunged over a 200-foot cliff and came to rest on its roof on the beach of a small cove. Richards was unconscious for three hours. When she came round she was able to find her mobile phone and use it to call the emergency services. The signal cut out six times and the operator had to keep calling her back. She was rescued later that morning.

Having broken up with her husband, the woman had a new boyfriend. But her ex-husband was stalking her, convinced that the woman's car was still his by rights. One night the woman and her new boyfriend came home by car without seeing a figure lurking in the shadows. As the boyfriend opened the passenger door, he was grabbed by the ex-husband, pulled out of the car and punched to the ground. The ex-husband ran round the other side of the car, pushed his ex-wife across to the passenger seat and drove away. The boyfriend picked himself up and, frantic with worry, phoned the police. Then he remembered that his girlfriend's bag was in the car and her mobile was switched on. The police were able to track the car by the mobile-phone signal. The ex-husband was arrested and charged with assault and car theft.

Other tracking uses include finding a doctor on the Orkneys and locating wandering patients who are suffering from suspected Alzheimer's Disease.

On the 192 bus.

'Hello . . . I'm on the bus . . . When did you phone? . . . Well, can you tell her I won't be coming in because I'm suffering.'

Woman on a bus.

'We're going past the request stop by the dry-cleaner's . . . No, you're thinking of the temporary stop by the launderette.'

(from Saul Barry, *She* magazine, September 1999)

One day in September 1999 a man was cycling in thick fog on the Kent coast. He cycled straight over a cliff at Bishopstone and plunged 50 feet to the beach below. Fortunately, he landed on soft mud and sand, and suffered only minor head and leg injuries. He phoned the coastguard on his mobile phone and a rescue operation was launched. A small fishing-vessel heard the man's cries for help and a lifeboat completed the rescue.

A young female cyclist stops at a red traffic light in Cambridge.

'Hello . . . Yes, brilliant . . . I'm calling because . . .'

And then no more was heard because the light had changed to green and she had cycled off one-handed while continuing to talk on the telephone. Another cyclist nearly ran into her and a bus driver just managed to overtake them both.

A woman is standing in the middle of the road.

'Hello, I want to report a fault on my house phone . . . Yes, a tree was blown over in last night's wind and it's pulled my phone-line down . . . It's in the middle of the road, in two pieces . . . No, I haven't tried my handset . . . I haven't tried my handset because I'm standing in the middle of the road next to the broken phone-line . . .'

A 43-year-old Norwegian man was kidnapped by masked men in Oslo. He was threatened with a gun, handcuffed and forced into the boot of a car. The kidnappers temporarily left the car on a secluded forest road. While they were gone, the man managed to reach his mobile phone and call the police. The connection was so bad that the police could hear only a few words. The key ones were 'kidnapped' and 'threatened' and the approximate location. The police found the man and rescued him.

(from the *Las Vegas Sun*, 8 October 1999)

Deborah Haynes, a businesswoman, was driving along the A16 near Boston, Lincolnshire, one afternoon in March 1998. She and her passenger, Susan Penny, had been visiting clients in South Lincolnshire. Haynes took a call on her mobile phone and talked to her boyfriend until they were cut off. She resumed the conversation with a second call and was arranging a dinner date when, driving with one hand, she pulled out at 70 mph to overtake a white pick-up truck. Her car crashed head-on with an oncoming vehicle. The driver of the oncoming vehicle was killed and Susan Penny was seriously injured. Haynes, who escaped with minor injuries, was later jailed for 12 months and banned from driving for two and a half years.

Heard on a bus.

'This is a call to all drivers – is there anybody out there who fancies volunteering for a bit of overtime?'

At 2.30 am on 4 April 1998, Mick Buffum fell asleep while driving on a quiet country road near Marilla, New York. His car went off the road and flipped on to its side. When Buffum

came round he heard a voice so he replied:

'The car's on its side . . . I can't get the door open.'

Without having made a phone call, Buffum found that he was talking to an emergency worker. Buffum's car had been fitted with an automatic emergency caller as part of its global positioning system. The system contained three crash senses that triggered on impact and relayed information about the car's location and the angle it was at. The emergency worker knew the car was on its side before Buffum had told him.

A bus pulls out of the bus station and immediately shunts into the back of a bus belonging to a rival company. The driver gets out and shuts in the passengers for 20 minutes while he argues with the other driver. Then he returns looking furious. A mobile phone rings near the front of the bus. The woman answers it in a whisper.

'We've been in an accident, but I can't talk too loudly because the driver's in a really bad mood.'

The rock-drummer Cozy Powell died in a road accident in April 1998. He was driving along the M4 while over the drink-driving limit and not wearing his seat-belt. He was talking to a girlfriend on his mobile phone at the time of the accident.

'I'm driving at 104 mph and I hope the engine doesn't seize, oh, shit . . .'

There was a loud bang as Powell's car spun out of control and hit the central reservation near Bristol.

In May 1998 a lorry driver contacted police on his mobile phone to say that he was careering south on the M1, at around 75 mph, in a 38-ton juggernaut and his brakes weren't working and the accelerator was jammed. Between Junction 11 and Junction 8 a siren-blazing police escort was put in place – one car in front of him and one behind – and a helicopter overhead. The police and the lorry driver stayed in touch by mobile phone. Eventually, after 20 miles, the lorry driver took police advice to turn off his engine, press the clutch, go down through the gears, steer on to the hard shoulder and bounce off the crash-barrier.

When police investigated the accident, they discovered that the lorry driver's background included a five-year prison sentence. While they accepted that the throttle had jammed and the engine was racing at a higher speed than normal, they suspected that the man had also been trying to attract attention to himself. They brought a case of dangerous driving against him. But after a six-day trial the driver was acquitted by the jury.

In September 1999 a 24-year-old woman was taking her driving test when she made an error at the Carville roundabout between Durham and the A1M Great North Road. Instead of taking a left turn down a minor road, she steered down the motorway slip-road. As learner drivers are banned from motorways (rule 227 of the *Highway Code*), this meant automatic test failure.

The examiner called for her to stop. Then, advising her to walk to the nearest SOS phone, he walked off himself. He knew that the insurance was invalid under such circumstances.

The driver (still a learner) reached for her mobile phone. Sobbing into the phone, she called the police and told them that her examiner had got out and walked away in the middle of her driving test. The police sent a patrol car to fetch her.

Driver of a four-wheel-drive vehicle after having been hit from the rear by another car.

'I have to hang up now, I'm having an accident.'

(from Latife Hayson, Lisa Tiver and Mark

Lynch, *Mobile Madness: A Guide to Mobile Phone Etiquette*, New Holland, 1997)

On a night in March 1999, Jonathan Baker, 39, drove towards his home in Devizes, Wiltshire. On the journey he talked to his ex-wife, Elizabeth Baker, on his mobile phone. At about 2 am he made a second call to his ex-wife. He asked to see her. He wanted to talk to her about his appointment with a psychiatrist the next day.

His car was near a village called Sixpenny Handley when his ex-wife heard a loud noise on the mobile phone. This was followed by quiet and muffled sounds. The car had left the road and hit a tree. The next words heard by Elizabeth Baker were uttered by someone else.

'Come on, mate, stay with us and we'll get you out of there.'

The phone sounded as if it was under water. Jonathan Baker was taken to a hospital in Salisbury but he died from head injuries.

On 1 September a Wiltshire coroner recorded a verdict of accidental death at the inquest.

Radelmeier and Tibhirani, two researchers from the University of Toronto, published research into the risks of mobile phones on the road in the *New England Journal of Medicine* (February 1997 issue). They found that drivers who possessed mobile phones were four times more likely to have accidents when using the phone than when not using the phone. Hands-free phones were no safer than hand-held phones. The risk was in the talking.

A 1997 study for the Rochester Institute of Technology, New York, found that the accident rate for drivers with car phones was 34 per cent higher than for those without.

Research commissioned by the Royal Society for the Prevention of Accidents (RoSPA) indicates that using a mobile phone at the wheel, whether hand-held or hands-free, greatly increases the likelihood of a driver having an accident. The dangers exist several minutes after a call while drivers are still mulling over a conversation, and the dangers are greater than those associated with talking to a passenger or tuning a car radio. Using a driving simulator, the study, conducted by the Psychology Department of the University of Aston, showed that drivers using a mobile phone were more stressed and less responsive to road and traffic conditions. The findings applied to drivers of manual- and automatic-transmission cars. A 1997 NOP Solutions public opinion poll showed that 84 per cent of people would like to see motorists banned from using hand-held mobile phones while driving.

Paragraph 127 of the 1999 Highway Code states: 'You MUST exercise proper control of your vehicle at all times. Never use a hand-held mobile phone or microphone while driving. Hands-free equipment is also likely to distract your attention from the road. It is safer not to use any telephone while you are driving – find a safe place to stop.'

The 1999 *Highway Code* also says, 'Never smoke or use a mobile phone on the forecourt of petrol stations as this is a major fire risk and could cause an explosion.' In case of breakdown on a motorway, it advises using the nearest motorway emergency telephone in preference to a mobile phone (unless you have a disability).

6

I'm in Town

A young woman is walking through the park on a romantic summer's day.

'I really can't stand that Tracey . . . Yeah, I know . . . Yeah, if I really wanted a shag I'd have a one-night stand, too, but she does it all the time.'

On the weekend of 7 August 1999, a man was killed in a Hamburg beer-garden. The victim's phone rang three times with an annoying melody. This led to three long conversations with friends. Another man in the beer-garden took umbrage at this and attacked the mobile-phone user with a beer bottle. The victim was clubbed to death with

repeated blows. Then the killer turned himself in.

(from Simon Hoggart, in the *Guardian*, 14
August 1999)

A young woman is wheeling a pushchair
across the market-place.

'It's me . . . What did Darren get? . . . Oh, bail
. . . Okay, well tell him I'll see him tonight
then.'

When Robert Monroe visited Chester in 1994
(letter to *The Times*, 15 October), he was de-
lighted to see a town crier in full regalia. The
town crier was striding purposefully along the
thoroughfare with his bell in one hand – and a
mobile phone in the other.

Man outside a pub looking through the pub window.

'It was too crowded in there . . . No, I couldn't find you . . . I'm at the window now.'

A young man wearing a NO NONSENSE T-shirt in a pub.

'. . . Yeah . . . When I had all that money in that account . . . It was just the look on the tellers' faces . . . I went in the bank and they said, "We need some ID off you," but the tellers said, "It's all right, we know him . . . Unmarked £5 notes . . . All in a carrier-bag . . ."'

Man in a shop doorway.

'. . . and the goalkeeper scooped it up and it went in the net and they won 2-1.'

In June 1999, a 22-year-old unemployed musician was ordered to pay £350 for smashing his former girlfriend's mobile phone and damaging her car.

David Alexander, writing in the *Guardian* about mobile phones in Italy (2 June 1999), describes a romantic scene in the Piazza San Giovanni. Two lovers stroll arm in arm. The man talks on the telephone with his right hand and the woman talks on her mobile phone with her left hand. Are they talking to each other?

Alexander has also noticed skiers in the Dolomites pausing in the middle of runs to answer the phone.

A young woman walks into a newsagency while talking on her mobile phone.

'Yeah . . . I'm just shopping [points to a packet of Marlborough cigarettes] . . . What are you doing tonight? [hands over money] . . . I'm always on the breadline, you know that . . .'

She takes the change and walks out.

A man is leaving the Old Trafford Football Stadium where Manchester United have been playing Southampton. After leading 3-1, Manchester United had conceded two late goals to draw 3-3.

'All right, yeah, so you know the fucking score.'

David Barnshaw was murdered in Stockport, Cheshire, on the evening of 20 September 1999. He was tortured in a car and burned alive. A mobile phone in the boot of the car was left with the line open on a call to police headquarters, allowing the police to record Barnshaw's screams. The line went silent when the car exploded.

A man with a dog is standing in a good spot in the city centre. 'Big Issue,' he says, 'Big Issue . . . help the homeless . . . Big Issue.' Then his mobile phone rings.

'Hello . . . oh, aye up, Daz . . . Yeah, I'll be back about five.'

Five people are standing outside the entrance to a university school of business. They are having an earnest academic discussion about the talk that they have just heard. A woman holding a mobile phone comes out of the door and walks through the group.

'Why are you laughing?'

A bit bemused, the five people stop their

conversation and watch the woman walk away. Then they resume.

A young woman is pacing uneasily outside a theatre for twenty minutes. She fiddles with her mobile phone.

'Hi, Helen . . .' She looks at mobile phone: 'Oh shit.'

The young woman tries again.

'Hi, Helen . . . Where are you? . . . Ha ha ha ha ha ha ha ha ha ha ha . . . I'll walk to you . . . About a minute . . . Just wait there.'

In Cambridge a woman holds a mobile phone to her left ear. A man stands on his left leg while his right foot is wedged two feet up a lamp-post. The man holds a notepad on his right thigh. The woman writes on the notepad with her right hand.

A young woman studies the catalogue in an Argos Store.

'Hello, it's me . . . I'm in Argos looking at these home haircutting kits . . . Yes . . . There's one at £14.99 and one at £8.99 . . . Babyliss. It's got clippers with adjustable, angled cutting head for fine cut adjustment and a comb and cleaning brush . . . No, it doesn't . . . The £8.99? . . . you reckon? . . . I think I'll get the other one . . . Yeah, and I've thought of another item for the wedding list . . . A wooden bowl for salads, one of those ones with wooden tongs . . . Yeah . . . Is he there by the way? . . . Has any washing-up been done? . . . No washing-up . . . Oh . . . I see . . . Okay, see you later then, Mummy.'

Brian Walker of Tadcaster, North Yorkshire, wrote to *The Times* (26 January 1999) to point out the wording of a sign in a Leeds mobile-phone shop: '100 minutes free calls – only £25.'

A queue is forming at a checkout in a small-town supermarket in Norfolk. The customers grow angry as the woman currently being served talks on her mobile phone.

'We're all going up to my sister's at Lynn. Why don't you come over when you've finished? Or are you seeing that Tony tonight?'
(from the *Guardian*, 12 June 1999)

A man stands in a shop doorway.

'All right then, mate . . . Yeah, see you then, mate . . . Bye-bye . . . Yeah, same to you . . . Bye-bye . . . Cheers . . . See you later then . . . Bye-bye . . .'

A woman in the Crossroads Shopping Mall, Salt Lake City, Utah.

'Well, first of all you must avoid corn starch . . . Hold on a minute, honey [fumbling in handbag] I'll just look in my handbook under "womb".'

A woman in a post office.

'That's funny, we were going to Malta in 1974 but then there was all that trouble with Saddam Hussein.'

A young girl in Marks & Spencer just before Christmas.

'It's me . . . What size socks did you say my dad takes?'

On the street during a crowded Mardi Gras Festival in Manchester.

'I'm round the corner from you . . . How do I know that? . . . Because I've just seen you round the corner.'

Man in a restaurant.

'Where are you? I'm in lunch.'

A couple are eating side by side in a restaurant. The woman has a bare midriff and heavily shadowed eyes. She snuggles up closely to her man. Then she excuses herself to go to the toilet. The man turns and watches her go. Then, when she is out of sight, he picks up his mobile phone and makes a call.

'Sherry? . . . Hi, babe . . . Just wanted to see how you're doing. I'm sitting here thinking about you.'

Woman in a café.

'I'm in Buxton . . . Buxton . . . I'm having the weekend here . . . It's only three-quarters of an hour from where I live . . . Wimslow. Where are you? . . . You're joking? . . . With Len? . . . Get to Buxton . . .What am I doing in Buxton? . . . In a hotel . . .Yes, she's fine, she's in Broadstairs this weekend . . . Broadstairs . . .It's down your way somewhere . . . No, no, a female . . . How long are you here for? . . . I can't hear you now . . . I can't hear you very well . . . I'm back home on Monday . . . Oh, right . . . Lovely to hear from you . . . Give my love to Len.'

A man is following his wife and small child into a restaurant.

'Okay, Digsy, okay, mate, do the deal.'

A couple from Silver Spring, Maryland, were dining in a restaurant in Laurel, Delaware, when a mobile phone rang on the next table. The woman who answered was obviously a medical professional. She dealt with a pregnancy emergency by setting up special treatment, in the course of which she even revealed the patient's name. After hearing her graphic descriptions of bodily fluids, the couple from Maryland lost their appetite completely.

(from Eve Zibart, in the *Washington Post*, 3 February 1999)

Man in blue overalls in a post office queue.

'Is it just checking the flue or is it to install it? . . . I see . . . Well, tell her that I can check the flue for free but it will be £45, no £48, to install it . . . plus VAT.'

In a café.

'I must brush up on my Javanese.'

Man in a pub.

'Who are they playing next week? . . . Oh, Walsall . . . Is that the Walsall in Russia or our Walsall?'

A woman is walking through a shopping precinct with a young child in a pushchair. She pushes the chair with one hand while she brings out her mobile phone. Then with no hands as she dials her number. Then she runs after the pushchair and wheels it with one hand while she talks on the phone.

A businessman in his fifties on the pavement of a busy city-centre street.

'I'm sorry, I missed that, I'm trying to negotiate a crossing . . . I'm sorry, I'm going to have to end this conversation now, I'm in danger of getting killed.'

The CAMRA *Beer Guide* for 2000 has an entry for a pub called The Hero of Switzerland in Loughborough Junction, London SW9. It includes the following sentence: 'The landlord will ask you to leave if your mobile phone rings in the bar.'

Man in blue anorak and red hard-hat, walking briskly along a city-centre street.

'I've just got to do what I've got to do now . . .

I'll come in the office after I've done what I've got to do now . . .'

Young lad leaning up against a lamp-post on a Monday afternoon.

'I was supposed to meet Claire yesterday afternoon but I couldn't be bothered . . . I was getting pissed the night before.'

It is late on a Saturday afternoon. A young man is jumping up and down outside a pub in the centre of a southern city. He is pointing the index finger of his right hand and repeatedly thrusting his arm through a 20-degree arc.

'You dirty fuckin' slag . . . When I get home I'm gonna beat the fuckin' shit outa you.'

Man in his forties or fifties, walking along a busy main street.

'I'll give you a ring when I'm on my way to pick you up . . . I just wanted to let you know about the weekend after next . . . All right my darling . . . Love you.'

And finally, here is evidence that mobile-phone stories may continue through future generations. A three-year-old girl is leaning back in her pushchair in an American household goods store called Crate and Barrel.

'Well, Grandma, it's always nice to talk to you.'